Library of
Davidson College

Library of
Davidson College

The Orchard Upstairs

The Orchard Upstairs

PENELOPE SHUTTLE

Oxford New York Toronto Melbourne
OXFORD UNIVERSITY PRESS
1980

Oxford University Press, Walton Street, Oxford OX2 6DP
London Glasgow New York Toronto
Delhi Bombay Calcutta Madras Karachi
Kuala Lumpur Singapore Hong Kong Tokyo
Nairobi Dar es Salaam Cape Town
Melbourne Wellington
and associate companies in
Beirut Berlin Ibadan Mexico City

© Penelope Shuttle 1980

All rights reserved. No part of this publication may be reproduced, stored in a retrieval system, or transmitted, in any form or by any means, electronic, mechanical, photocopying, recording, or otherwise, without the prior permission of Oxford University Press

This book is sold subject to the condition that it shall not, by way of trade or otherwise, be lent, re-sold, hired out, or otherwise circulated without the publisher's prior consent in any form of binding or cover other than that in which it is published and without a similar condition including this condition being imposed on the subsequent purchaser.

British Library Cataloguing in Publication Data
Shuttle, Penelope
The orchard upstairs.
I. Title
821'.9'14   PR6069.H80/   80-40854
ISBN 0-19-211938-9

Printed in Great Britain by
The Bowering Press Limited
Plymouth

To Peter, and to our daughter Zoe
To my mother and father, Joan and Jack

Contents

Eavesdropper	1
The Dancer	2
Skeletals	3
Three Lunulae, Truro Museum	4
Ghost	6
Past Injuries	7
Rain	8
Appletree in America	9
Honesty	10
Downpour	11
Glass-Maker	12
Winter Train Journey	14
The Songbook of the Snow	16
Hot and Cold	22
November Poppies	23
Candle on a Rainy Morning	24
Four American Sketches	25
Cupboard Hyacinths	27
Travelling	28
The Silver Bridge	30
The Pale Places	31
Vehement Ceremony	32
'The World has Passed'	33
Fosse	35
Period	37
At Perranporth, March 1976	42
The Conceiving	44
Expectant Mother	45
First Foetal Movements of my Daughter, Summer 1976	46
The Dream	47
The Orchard Upstairs	49

Acknowledgements

Some of these poems first appeared in the following magazines and anthologies: *The Arts Council Anthology of New Poetry*, no. 2, P.E.N. Anthologies *New Poems 1973/74, 1974/75 and 1976/77; Xenia, Matrix, The Scotsman, Poetry Review, Poetry Book Society Christmas Supplement 1978, Meridian, Bananas, Pink Peace*; and some have previously appeared in pamphlets and broadsheets published by the Sceptre Press, Janus Press, Headland Publications, Words Press and The Quarto Press.

Acknowledgements are also due to Routledge & Kegan Paul Ltd for the poems 'Candle on a Rainy Morning' and 'Travelling', which first appeared in *The Terrors of Dr Treviles*, a novel, by Peter Redgrove and Penelope Shuttle, 1974.

The BBC Radio 3 (Bristol) Westward Look programme first broadcast the poem 'Three Lunulae, Truro Museum', and BBC 3 'Poetry Now' first broadcast 'The World has Passed'.

Eavesdropper

Here is your face
wintering in a photograph,
alive and alone

I look at it,
at you as you were then,
and the midsummer opens,

pale feathers of ice fall
from the sky around me
and nearby, the ocean,

like a ghost's throat,
grows translucent.

The Dancer

Look, a dancer stuck between the moon
and the earth. She can't get away
from her terrible stage scenery,
cruel and unchanging. It gives no guidance.
Why is she stitched so tight
into this dance, with her bony ribbons
and miser's lace?

Look, the dancer gets up speed,
her stopwatch in her hand.
Her steps are several miles distant
from her heart.
This dancer is waiting for a listener.
Earth and moon grow stronger,
she is ebbing, the sluttish memoir of the tide
pulls her. Her feet hammer down
on the stage, a frost of foreign currency.
At last she lifts her arms, pauses,
hesitation of the translator.
And comes, like lace, like ice,
to a standstill, at the edge of an ammunition,
her frail geography barely remembered
except as a swift erasure of shadows.

Skeletals

Three skeletals are climbing
out of their blue and gold boxes.
They lift the lids of their coffins
and clamber out, naked,
each ribcage a cuirass of bone.
The central corpse
lifts up his arms in astonished blessing.
Behind him,
a tapestry of three-petalled flowers
flourishes,
trinity behind trinity.

And the celebration goes on,
the joyful pillage of golden light,
the rescue from a long deep dark,
the arrival into unfading colour
from the fastness of the sepulchre.

Three Lunulae, Truro Museum

Gold so thin,
only an old woman
would notice its weight

Crescent moons of gold
from the sunken district
of the dark,
out of the archaeologist's earth

The women of the lunulae
threw no barbaric shadows
yet a vivid dance
lit up their bones

I sense the mood
of many women
who wore the new moon
like a necklace

They have got over
the winter
while I still freeze

The slight quick tap
of a clock
goes on
like the rhythm
of an insect's leg
in the grass

I linger
in the locked room
of the gold,

trying to see,
beyond the sickle shapes,
the faces of three women

Sharp shadows breathe hard,
shedding skins like dusty snakes
Light twists in a violent retching

For an instant
there is the fragment of a lip,
an eyebrow fine as a spider's threat

A face like a frost fern

The custodian
locks the lunulae
in the safe once more

Cornish, they are,
he says,
dug up at St Juliot,
regalia of this soil,
and not for the British Museum

You buy me
a postcard of the lunulae
and we leave the museum,
enter the thin gold remains
of autumn

Ghost

Ghost:
a state of being shaken,
cold vibration, trembling fields,
shadows of snow

My ghost:
whose smile resembles soft slate,
whose statements, promises, answers
are of doubtful integrity

My ghost who travels in a ramshackle conveyance,
who defers indefinitely the embrace
I ask of her

My ghost who moves like lightning
in wide extended flashes
I will one day smash you in many bright empty pieces of frost
or at least pare off a thin cold slice of you

Shall send you below the horizon,
turn you back to odds and ends,
make you less than loose fragments of rock
on a steep slope,
an illegible and torn letter
and not my ghost

But not yet
Like the white bird against the dark sky,
you must still move against my life

A repatriation, not a haunting . . .
Ghost putting me to rights again

Past Injuries

Forgotten now, that labour and other pains
on this mild day of winter sun.
Soon the winter solstice
will astonish me and the hilly fields beyond the town.

The sea moves calmly.
It is steadfast, its colours are lawful.
Yet a combination of circumstances
can easily drive the ocean mad.

I think again of a day and a night lost
in the fire of my child's coming.
Is it time yet to contemplate
that part of the picture long hidden?

No. This is calm sun between pains.
This is where I rest on the journey,
read the pastel page of the book,
dream of one of the remote planets of the sun.

Rain

There is the thunder again
The rain falls
on the houses full of bags of bones
No one cuts flowers
The empty promises of the month
flush down beneath the streets,
through drains
The dots and dashes of the rain
are a waterlogged code

I am in the conscript army of summer
The rain dowses my fingerprints
Roses shudder, even the limbs of trees ache

On the shelf, the books are stern as cloud
I cannot read them

The rain stands miles apart from all the bibles
overcoming words with its own saturating argot

Appletree in America

An appletree by the roadside
and the road five hours travelling
out of New York City.

Here's a frontier,
this tree ripening
and the windfalls on the ground
like a first furnishing
in a continent
where I flit like a ghost
unanchored at twilight.

I hold a branch
and smell the apples,
watersweet, a beginning,
opening of energies
to rouse me from homesickness
as, beyond the roadside tree,
these foreign fields and hills
merge into the familiar loam of evening.

Honesty

What are these papery flowers,
thin stiff petals dry as insects,
these plants that rustle

as I pick them? Dry dilemmas,
arranged in a glass of water,
they go on puzzling me.

For days they are quite still,
unchanging.
They will not move in any breeze.

I see these nameless oval wafers
as if in an offing,
the most distant part of the sea
visible from the shore.

But when I touch their dry membranes,
they do not resist,
only fade and disintegrate,
finding the end of their pallor.

They are not unapproachable.
My mother says they are called 'honesty'.

Downpour

A strong rain falls, a bony downpour.
The waters roar, like a riddance.
The day vanishes suddenly
and it is night that hesitates on a brink
for fear of difficulties. The rain, for instance.

Through the letter box, leaves instead of letters,
wet leaves blown along the path
and seeping through the low letter box,
an invasion that comes slowly,
but helped by the rain. The downpour.

I dream of thorns, aeroplanes and red horses,
but seldom of rain.
The creature spinning webs to catch its prey,
I dream of her also
but almost never of rain. The webs of rain.

The rain does not slacken. It has the scent
of mistletoe. But it is a weapon, thrown.
The windows shine black with it.
I sit watching the knotted bunches of rain.
I do not want to cease watching. Such brawny rain.

But the dry house, its music and its meals,
recalls me from the window,
draws me back from a downpour that is drowning me.
I prepare to turn from the window,
yet remain a moment longer,
looking at the blur of the candle-flame
against the dark glass.

There is the downpour. Here is the uprush of light.

Glass-Maker

It is no skill of mine,
glass-making.
I apprehend none of its craft,
transparency wiser than gardens.

To make glass
is clearer communication than speech.
A woman-maker of windows,
how would she look?

Angrily, piercingly at you
through her own upstairs window?
Or would she be smooth, hairless,
all bone, glabella?

Arduous manufacture, glass,
yet so simple to break.
Just strike it a glancing blow
and see the fragments, petal-less.

Are there glass-makers
on Arcturus or Aldebaran?
Does sun there sheer off unknown windows,
create blinding mirrors?

Dress me in glass!
Shoes, sleeves, all . . .
Let me move with great care,
interned in glass garments,
until I become glass,
my body made of glass,
cool and irreversible change,
glass eyebrow,
fingernail, clitoris . . .

Bone, blood and breath: all glass.
Until I am a devotee of glass,
reflecting all its famishings.

Winter Train Journey

First Window
The fields of frost,
the shed roof
white with cold,
the blackberries
frozen on the bushes

Shadow of a white bird
on the brown water

Second Window
The amazingly green fields
from which the frost
has just melted

The two black and white bullocks
climbing the slope to the edge of the thin trees

Third Window
Five oak trees
across a field of frost
The dead man
does not see this landscape
Sheep move
across the field
that hovers its colour
between white and green

Fourth Window
Webs of cold
matt the grasses
The sun, between autumn and winter,
fingers each oak leaf,
as if disbelieving such shades,
so many languages of colour

Fifth Window
One ridge of the valley
is green, without frost
The other, out of the early sun's reach,
remains white with the frost frill
The moon takes one last look
from the half of itself that remains,
then fades
in a flurry of magpies

Sixth Window
White smoke
from the rubbish heap
and the last
of the morning mist
move out in
skirls over the huge river

i.m. B.S. Johnson

The Songbook of the Snow

1
Twilight
A fistful of feathers
An indefinite length of time

Difficulty in speaking
Cold downfall of daffodils

2
Swart snowclouds:
the winter sunlight
gutters out like a candle

3
Ambushes of cloud
Cold muddle of after-snow
Air
    cold as a creed
Impediments of ice

4
In winter
love
is kept partly below
the surface
so that it might take root

5
Casual words
in a sidestreet
shatter my day
like glass
or ice on a pond
when a child throws
a stone

6
Bird-calls
signalling snow

An hour later,
the snow

Ice-coloured flowers for the peninsula

7
The winter midwife's darkness
is more acid than lemons

Her big red hands deny
the colours of flowers

8
A small field
enclosed by kitchen gardens of ice
warns the river
of the sour sharp stars

9
Tulips are waddling
in the cold orchards,
in touch with the snow

10
On Tuesday morning
the whisper of the cold
began again,
the scent of the north pole

11
Candle-sticks and remembrance-books
belong to the winter

The gillyflower dictionary
has no answer
to the snow

12
The unicorns do not mind the snow
Snow is their life colour
The unicorns lose no desire amid the snow
Winter is their white pleasure-garden

13
A new candle eases
the weariness of winter
The old candle bowed down
beneath the cold
but the new stem basks
on the wintry windowsill
Behind the flame, snow is falling

14
Prisoners are born in winter
and have no memory of sun
The white frost forests
and the muddy snow
are where they end and begin

15
I carry the parcels of ice
I am the pedlar of snow
I am the walking winter

16
False coins of winter:
the albino woman stops
counting her money,
looks up at the moon

17
The snow is afraid
See! I thrust my finger into the snow
The snow sweats

18
Sabbath of snow
The footpath yields up tracks,
confessions of travellers

Ice is on the crucifixes

19
The snow goddess
hesitates
She limps to the fence
singing to an audience of cloud

20
The employees of the philosopher
have been locked out
of the library
and are shivering in the snowy courtyard

21
It is snowing
I might have learnt that language of snow
had I not feared the cold

22
The island you come from
is a winter island –
look at any map

23
The colours of snow –
grey, slate-blue, smoke –
refuse to budge
More snow falls
Pampered arrows of ice
vaguely heard in night sleep

Seagulls ransack the snowclouds angrily
The sunlight has been blown away, inland

And snow falls
and falls
like work carelessly done

24
The bed is not made yet, because of the snow
The floors are unswept, because of the snow
The girl is not married yet, because of the snow
The jokes do not sound right, because of the snow
The stars are just splinters now, because of the snow
The women are calm now, because of the snow
The avenues are blocked now, because of the snow
The high-schools are empty now, because of the snow
The soldiers are dying now, because of the snow
The daylight is strong now, because of the snow

It is northlight that rules now, because of the snow
Dreamlight and northlight, because of the snow
The blue jackdaw is free now, because of the snow
The alphabet is all now, because of the snow

Hot and Cold

Flags of fire that break
like saints' days,
spumes of red,
avowals of the heat.

In the cold my body aches.
Careless of consequences,
I dream of more flame-flags,
conjure up hot fortifications.

A plurality of wives is a coldness.
A tree and its fruits,
especially if a pomegranate,
is like a flame.

In the interval between contraction
and dilation of my hot heart,
I shiver.
All pearls are both hot and cold.

November Poppies

I post my letters
and turn from the town,
from the wild children
in the schoolyard,
to the sea
and the first darkness
coming down on the water,
down from the harbour hill
unstoppable
like a young rider
clinging to the back
of his terrified horse.
The hills across the bay
are the colour of slate roofs,
blue and grey,
and watching them I hear
the winter earth echoing,
I hear it reading its sun and moon letters.
Again the twilight wind
menaces the water.
I open my mouth to taste its coldness
that leaves no poison on my tongue.

An hour later, I open my door.
I hope for a friend to join me,
to talk and joke.
But it is a stranger on the threshold,
an old woman with envious eyes
lifting towards me her reproachful tray,
offering me hundreds of poppies,
the reek of remembrance.

Candle on a Rainy Morning

Raindark, a morning of thin magic
My room is lost beneath the shadows
of the family tree,
dilemmas of leaf, branches budding with memories
How can I pilgrimage beneath this blind and deaf tree
with its foliage of riches?

My room is the family forest
The skins of the window-pane shudder
Veiled aunts smile, chill and tardy
I can't sing or write my letters
The leaves are whispering like mother and father
My brother's laughter warns me from the topmost branches

What danger? I ask
What danger?
He laughs and points down at me
I see the red feathers sprouting from my wound

I stand by the window
The flame of the candle is thoughtful,
a poor relation
The trees do not shed leaves but family photographs
The smiles litter the floor
Pressed flowers fall from the pages of my notebook

These dry handfuls of summer have the pallor of unwound
    clocks
It is noon and I am feverish, thinking
of the strangers from whom I inherit the family forest
Last night I dreamt of holy and royal infants
Now the rain falls yellow as yesterday
Again the trees are part of the ugly wallpaper
The sky lightens, makes my candle redundant,
leaves me watching the finger of flame embark
upon the sunlight, perplexed, shut up in childhood.

Four American Sketches

The Blind
The sun outstares me.
I pull down the blind.
Under these old afternoon clothes
my scarf-skin quivers.
My skin is thin and dry
like certain plants
and I fear the approach of my stronger self,
that reflection
who will flay me
until the flaps of my skin
bang like blinds
in a wind that doesn't care.

One of the Narrations
These shrubs are unmarred by autumn.
A thousand narrations
might spring from their neighbourliness,
by my window.

But the shadow of my opponent
who wears my own inaccurate face
reaches out from unexpected hiding places,
ending my repose,
dragging me to sad locations
on the other side of the candle.

Here the autumn hobbles me.
All is cloudiness and the antagonist's hug.
We are face to face, she and I.
My dark side is towards the earth.

That New Moon
That new moon waiting for me
to step out into twilight
is no desolate island:

Not that little moon
around which the minnowy-blue sky flows,
no.

Nor is that new moon
made of snow.

That moon has the strength of a million spines.
It is this moon alone which stays awake all night.

November First, New York State
Spurges, cascarilla, cassava:
the steepings of November,
mild disrobings, a damp natural air,
a day of reprieve.
A sour cold waits its turn
but today the mazes of autumn revolve.
Our personal effects are wedged into bright rooms,
the windows are wide open,
breathing the almost extinct summer.
You and I are reading the bibliotheca of autumn.

Cupboard Hyacinths

In the cupboard under the stairs
the winter flowers are crooning
in their cardboard pots.

In the fierce dark
the roots of the hyacinth are stretching
their green havoc.

I sit on the stairs
thinking of the garden beneath me
in the underworld of the cupboard.

I think how handsome
my hyacinths will be,
how they will tower over December
with a fragrance as heavy as Isis.

I will keep their corms from pestilence
because they contain my answers.
Without the bending Pisas of their stems
I will have too many questions.

I wait by the cupboard door,
I want to hear them grow,
I want to experience the cupboard's weather.

I want to carry my blossoming lamps
into the winter rooms,
their odour a guttural equilibrium
settling everything once and for all.

Travelling

Across blue fields to find Satan
White stars above me, roots of fire
I want to unlock the keys of the piano

On volcanic islands I hear the passage
of clumsy adults without wings
I am one of them

Rain falls, many delicate colours
appear in the distance
Satan throws winter across his shoulder

I climb the hodden-gray hills
From the harbour I hear the hoarse
tender warning of the foghorn

There are no dinosaurs drinking
at the river's edge
I stoop, I throw a handful of red earth
into the river
There is no time to write a treatise
on this subject

I looked for Satan in the polar lands
My breath stood solid in the air
Cold seized me by the throat, made me helpless
But I did not find Satan,
could not touch his fiery rank flesh

I laboured in a summer garden
Women and children dressed in garish red garments
watched me

In their hands, they held bunches
of flowers, feathers and branches
Four women came towards me,
they related reminiscences to me until dusk,
and the children sat on the lawn, watching

I stand at the door of the granary
I snuff up the odours of harvest
Behind me, Satan is looking for his women
His jaw opens, extends into a beak
I walk to the edge of a steep place
I am looking down into the second sign of the zodiac
Darkness grows up in black clusters around me

But I step back from that edge
I enter a different darkness, it is the dark of the barn,
the sweet stench of the grain

The Silver Bridge

The child ran across the silver bridge,
across the river bridge, high and dangerous,
the same both ways, like a palindrome.

The child ran across the silver bridge
into smaller and thinner distance.
In its loose coat that flapped, it ran,
and its shadow skipped across the grey waters below.

In my hand I hold a key
that will not open the child's heart.
From the height of the bridge,
its thoughts reach out to me longingly.

The child has crossed the bridge.
It stands on the opposite bank, watching me.
The child's shadow is a sleek full blue.
The child has gone first, to clear the way for me.

Mournful and mild, I set my foot
on the silver bridge.
The bridge buckles, there is a shriek
of silver metals.

The first touch of my weight pulls
the bridge down. I fall, spiralling
down to the bony waters, the key in my hand.
The outrider, the child, watches me.
Our glances coincide in air, two curves meeting.
The child is expressionless.
I enter the water, amid pangs like a birth.

The Pale Places

The pale places of the candle
are available,
the prongs of light
change colour, arouse
the more delicate, the more disquieting hues.

I am midway through a month.
I am writing with my left hand,
a pale skiff going across the page.
I am divided into branches of blood,
their roots in polar earth.

A slight breeze moves in and out of my lungs.

I want to go with the moon,
palest of places.
But after sunset, when creatures
set about their thieving,
I fear I shall be left behind,
my blood heavy like an unshed husk,
a burden for me to carry alone,
a refrain of tonnage,
a weight I don't want to bear,
encumbrance that is stiffening
all of the light.

Vehement Ceremony

Vehement ceremony,
detonation!

Branched, forked blood
My leave of absence cancelled

Contrapuntalist deep in me,
these fugues gushing

Funicular of red flowers,
tactless fuel pouring away

A rose
wounded, scorched and stupefied

Hydraulic that forces me down
into the hyssop veins of my uterus

'The World has Passed'*

On the other side of the rose
there is the felling of trees

On the other side of the frost
there is the colour of a bruise

On the other side of the ovum
there is the woman of warfare

On the other side of the bonfire
there is the music springing back,
the retaliation

On the other side of the leaf
is the lesson in lacemaking

On the other side of the room
is a cabinet of curiosities, antique granary

On the other side of the mother
is a sigh full of filaments,
a few words walking on tiptoe

On the other side of the blackberry
is the harvest of the moon

On the other side of the voice
is the absence of the waterfall

On the other side of the ice
is the half-satisfied sea

On the other side of the blood
is the unrooted child

On the other side of the child
is the gulping-down of cloud,
the whispering of loopholes –
arrival at last at the fresh shrine

*Yokut, American-Indian term for 'a year has gone by'.

Fosse

> '... and from the menstrual ditch
> The future runs...'
> – Peter Porter, 'Three Bagatelles'

I am always on the brink.
As one beginning is dwarfed
and changes colour, reddens,
dies, in fact,
and makes for the dark easement
of earth
that is its and my past,
a blindness of words and counties,
I am at the precipice,
listening secretly to that whisper,
the promise of rank,
the possibility of passwords.
Always on the edge,
always at the frontier,
waiting until my papers are in order,
until I can emigrate.
But I am not authorized yet.
Today I learnt that my key
did not unlock the clasp,
that the combination was not perfect
enough to open the deeply-implanted safe.
So I go on waiting here,
in this embrasure of autumn,
prepared for emergencies.
I am here to correct my mistakes.
These corrections are made in blood,
on the borderland of riddles,
at the brink of encyclopedias
I cannot open and read yet.
I accept the repetition
that is always different,

I accept the enclave of the month.
In my deep roots,
the engrossment of my blood aches,
it is cancelling out
the enchantment I planned
and offering a famine.
Yet it offers other habits.
Its perceptions are a new clarity,
the red geraniums, the yellow sunflowers
throb with beauty and versatility.
This blood is a real thing in itself.
It has its heirs and settlements.
In its environment I cannot proclaim
my hostility for long.
No sooner has the month's answer come,
been feared, hated and then accepted,
danced with, adored,
than the fallow hesitations of myself
are audible again,
I hear the new question and its invitation.
Bleeding this fathomless blood,
I move to the brink again,
joyful, beginning again, celebrating:
the new sputters in me
like a fire trying to catch,
it flickers and burns unsteadily,
jerks like a volley of red arrows.

I wait, on the brink of the blaze.

Period

One
Waterfall (of legendary bone)
blood manuscripts
A seed of melancholy, a blind red lizard
belonging to me

Night bird of red
and a morning handled roughly
Fatigue, deity of darkness

I ache without eggs
My belly is an extinct door
The red pinnacles hurt
The brink of my forehead is cold
        blue accents are there

Bleak trees on a slanting bank

I shiver because of my scarlet cargo

Wan language I speak unwillingly

The reprimands twine, prolonging the dark

Go away, this is too much moon,
soaking my underclothes,
hodding my day with weariness

The greenery of the forest has gone grey
I am married to a whirlpool
Seaweed is my mirror

I was on the watch for this late blood so long
that I grew tired and forgot it

and now it accosts me roughly,
and addles my little knowledge to nothing
Pages I try to read are dark charcoal maps,
too smudged to see the paths

And I carry ghost in my boggy place,
embryo of the moon,
diaphanous, filamentous, water transport

The white is stained with sticky reds
Two or more figures are gathering
in the thin mortar of twilight
and they attempt to find something in the dark –
me, perhaps?

The blood hoists its pains
My exclamation, my warning to stop
is ignored
My words float down to the humus
of the hills

I move in an inward direction
I love Horae
Between my bones, the leaves catch and jolt me
My own lunar crater is deep and untidy today

What do I make of this pain and confusion,
this mania of sadness,
my unsteady steps

Is it a long story?

Two
Stiff feathers of the womb,
they pain me
as they turn into blood

How can I tell of this pain,
this dark between my pelvic bones,
this shadow in my mind,
how can I relate it?

I am bloated with blood
that pours and pours from me
as fast as the rush of blood
in the flock of birds that sweeps across
the sky and out over the river

I am wet with this sediment,
this pulp of womb, this mess of moon

And it will happen again
Again I will wake from sleep
with the pain counting its stitches
across me, at all compass points,
and I will know I am depicted as broken

It is a ghost that moves with a crunching sound
bones and ice
and at first it was kind
and I smiled on the first day of the blood,
was gay, growing riper

But on the second day of my period,
I am climbing the hazardous part of the stairs
My body has shrunk, is wrinkled,
and my sluggishness
has only the expression of a single idea:
dark pain through chinks of the bag

Three
Like a root torn up,
I bleed
my brief outburst of joy is over
Now I find fault with this blood
I do not want this opportunity,
this outlook

For the past month,
I have been exploring
the landscape of a woman,
the menstrual fields

What did I look for?
The shape of the moon,
the darting fragments of planets,
my own face in clean mirrors,
true houses in which to live:

but at the end of the exploration
no answers and no blood came:
the balance was not found
I heard a faint indistinct song
and that was all

I turned from the landscape of the month
and became feverish,
my voice dried in my mouth
I swallowed thorns and my throat was torn
I was weak from the combat

Yesterday morning I awoke early,
frightened by the noose tightening around my hips
As I rose from the bed, the oozy flow
stuck my nightdress to my thighs
I was happy then

Today the trouble is too much blood,
gushing, spouting from me,
leaving my body empty, clumsy and tired
I slant idly into the day
I am down in the dark, amid the spoors of my blood

It is long since the bleeding was so hard,
long since I was so rent by the stride of the blood,
since I felt burst by a flood and was afraid

I dreamt, two weeks ago,
of the bloody holy hole
Now I am riding on that red palfrey
and the reins have cutting edges

There on the ground! A splash of blood
From my wounded hands? Or from the deep
and wrenched tide of me?

At Perranporth, March 1976

On the cliffpath that March,
where the primroses veined the turf
and the water hesitated
to bruise its skin on the rocks,
beneath the sky of low cloud
reaching down to the dunes,
we walked in the late afternoon,
on the very edge of the land.

Behind us, the empty and echoless
shafts of worked-out tin mines,
tunnels inching out mortally
under the seabed.
Now the ocean eavesdrops
but hears nothing, the men dead
who worked in the flowerless dark
beneath the sea,
and nothing, not even a whisper
of arrears remains.

The path is narrow,
we go cautiously, in single file.
The horizon is putting an end to the day.
No ships, no sunset,
only the white cloud and the grey sea
twined together to make evening.
We reach the second headland
and see the cliffpath
descending into the long silent vowels of twilight.

The wind blows up,
makes our way more difficult,
the strong breeze pulling at coats

and hair, tilting us off balance
and we scramble to the higher wider path.

You say,
in that wind I hear stone horsemen
riding across these cliffs.
As we came closer to the town fields
I heard the far-off calling voices
of children playing
and one indistinguishable sound,
repeated and repeated,
a child calling to a friend,
and though I listened hard, urgently,
I could not make out that name,
uttered again and again,
persistent and without malice,
a long cooing note, the sound of twilight.

I thought then
it was like the voice of the sea or the evening,
calling to life my child
and naming it,
and though no sign arose yet from my body,
I sensed within me
the days-old life
that now in summer grows larger in me,
veined and shining in the waters of me,
that Mare Serena, Uterina.

The Conceiving
(for Zoe)

Now
you are in the ark of my blood
in the river of my bones
in the woodland of my muscles
in the ligaments of my hair
in the wit of my hands
in the smear of my shadow
in the armada of my brain
under the stars of my skull
in the arms of my womb
Now you are here
you worker in the gold of flesh

Expectant Mother

In the stillness,
uterine,
hidden from me,
hidden from mirrors,
the foetal roots of wrist
and heart
are coiled within me.
They belong to the child,
to the incast,
a plumage of constellations.

I walk around the house
in bare feet
and a warm rope of blood
links me to my child

Rain falls on gardens and inscriptions
but I hold the edge of the rain.
I am a receptacle
in which other rain, amniotic, gathers,
for the one in his official residence
to enjoy.

I think of the quiet use of the unborn eyelids
and the stillness of my breasts that swell up,
a warm procedure of strength.

Already a name suggests its syllables,
but this remains secret,
a fishtail shadow,
a whisper between the night and the day.

First Foetal Movements of my Daughter, Summer 1976.

Shadow of a fish
The water-echo
Inner florist dancing
Her fathomless ease
Her gauzy thumbs
Leapfrogger,
her olympics in the womb's stadium

The Dream

In my dream, I was deaf.
He touched my ear in friendship
but when he felt my deafness,

the ball of wax blocking my hearing,
he turned sadly away
leaving me alone in the dark foreign room.

This morning I listen to music
and recall the muffled dream,
his soundless footsteps on the paved floor.

I wonder what deafness lurks in me,
what handicap waits for my acknowledgement?
What wisdom have I closed my ears to?

What thoughts dishevelled between the old
and the new moon, what dishfuls of fear,
what enemy actions did he perceive, touching my ear?

I am unable to forget the dream's broken message,
have no splints to mend it.
I will not deprive myself of its warning.
All day I listen for the inauguration of my deafness.

The haze of dream is only the beginning.
Unless I travel to the right bondage,
I may never hear the word the dream wants to say,
never hear the word that will reshape my life.

And all the nights of dream to come
will be reproach, mouths uttering and no sound coming,
questions asked and answers given and I unable
to interpret any of these riches.

As I write
I feel again that touch of a hand against my ear,
a secret and strong act.
I believe the touch that discovered my deafness

also cured the blemish,
that my hindrances are temporary:
I believe that the gesture of warning is also a blessing.

I was locked into a silence of my own manufacture
but am now emerging free,
clear of the boundaries, out amid the bivouacs of cold,
listening hard to all weathers.

The Orchard Upstairs

1
Here I meet no king-killer
Here I throw no shadow
Before birth, before the present tense,
I moved here amid darks, lunar dusk,
a ferret of blood, the unborn,
fenestella

2
Outside, the wind and the rain,
a darkness lurching against the threadbare house:
inside, the orchard upstairs

But I do not understand these fruits yet

3
Around the moon,
my dreams cluster, not moths
The antique photographs of the dreams
lead me always to this one room,
overlooking neglected lawn and pond
From a window I look down again
at the leafy air-raid shelter,
hear again steam trains shunting beyond the trees

Opening a door to a room in which apples are stored
in rows, I hear the stark cries of a woman giving birth

4
The room was cold, as if no glass
were fixed in the window frames
The room was damp, as if a fountain
sprang in the centre of the room
The room was draughty,
as if the house was fallen in ruins

I stand at the threshold,
lunar observer at the brink of apples

5
In the unused room
she laid out the windfall apples in rows
The silent house was filled with the scent of bruised apples
I climb the stairs
of a familiar house whose demolition approaches
My bones break with the bricks,
the foundations of my heart will crack

6
Something, a cloth, a veil?
chokes me
The doorways throb, like yew branches
in a storm
The old house eavesdrops
It bewails my thoughts

7
I do not sleep in this bedroom any more
But I shed skins here
I touch the skin of an apple
It is smooth as the ear of a hare

8
A woman in childbirth,
the difficult fame of labour
All night, all day, all night again:
the freshly-painted walls of the nursery
echo with her whorling cries

At dawn, a newborn howling amid
the apples of the future

9
The leaves scud before the wind
across the lawn,
leaves like birthmarks

10
A small speck or stain
on my heart,
it is my sadness for the lost room,
the pillaged house

What are the conditions for equilibrium?
Is there a balance among apples?

11
Like bone the stairs that I climb
and ice the banisters I grasp
Is it a garden of fruit trees I approach,
or is it a cemetery
   And the brightness of colour,
      is it life or death,
         that red?

12
In the morning, the sun cools itself
against the orchard mirror
I sit on the window ledge
and below me the lawn is calm green water,
a lake of old love

LIBRARY OF DAVIDSON COLLEGE